I LIKE this BOOK

I LOVE this BOOK

# SUPER STRUCTURES OF THE WORLD

# BOEING 747

**BLACKBIRCH®**
**PRESS**

**THOMSON**
**GALE**

San Diego • Detroit • New York • San Francisco • Cleveland • New Haven, Conn. • Waterville, Maine • London • Munich

LIBRARY OF CONGRESS CATALOGING-IN-PUBLICATION DATA

Boeing 747 / Bruce Glassman, book editor.
    p. cm. — (Super structures of the world)
Summary: Examines the history of the world's largest and fastest commercial jet, the Boeing 747-400, including some of the challenges faced in design and construction and how its builders tested the limits of technology.
Includes bibliographical references and index.
    ISBN 1-56711-864-X (hardcover : alk. paper) — ISBN 1-4103-0191-5 (pbk. : alk. paper)
    1.  Boeing 747 (Jet transports)—Juvenile literature. [1. Boeing 747 (Jet transports)
    2. Jet planes.]  I. Glassman, Bruce. II. Series.

TL686.B65B56 2004
629.133'349—dc21                                                        2003007097

Printed in China
10 9 8 7 6 5 4 3 2 1

# BOEING 747-400

The Boeing 747 is the biggest commercially built passenger aircraft in the world. It is built in the biggest building in the world. It carries the president of the United States. It ferries the space shuttle. It will soon blast missiles out of the sky with a laser. It has flown 15 million flights totaling 35 billion miles—equal to seventy-four thousand trips to the moon and back. And as this mighty jet dominates the skies, it makes the world a smaller place.

But this jet is more than the sum of its staggering dimensions. The 747 has a mythical stature. Cutting-edge technology, the passion of the people who build it—these are some of the elements that combine to make the story of the Boeing 747 a tale of testing the limits, then flying far beyond them.

## BIGGEST AND FASTEST

They say first impressions are everything. And one thought pops into anyone's mind the first time they encounter a Boeing 747: This airplane is huge. Even the people who work with the jet day in and day out remain stunned by its size.

The awesome dimensions of the 747-400, the current version of the jet, dwarf every other commercial jet in production. This jet is 231 feet, 10 inches long. If someone could manage to stand a 747 on its tail in Seattle's Safeco Field, the stadium's retractable roof would need to be open because the jet's nose would poke out of the ballpark about fifteen feet.

*Above: More than 231 feet long and with a wingspan of fifty-six hundred feet, the Boeing 747-400 dwarfs every other commercial jet in existence.*

*Left: The jet is so big that if it were raised vertically to stand on its tail, it would extend fifteen feet above the highest seats of a sports stadium.*

The 747-400's wings cover fifty-six hundred square feet. They could serve as a parking lot for forty-five midsize cars. And when this jet is filled to its capacity with fuel, the wingspan grows. Full tanks pull the wings down slightly, and the span grows from 211 feet to 213. The jet's cockpit sits 29 feet above the ground. The empennage, or tail section, tops out at 63 feet, the height of a five-story apartment building. Fully fuelled and loaded to capacity, the 747-400 can weigh up to 875,000 pounds.

*Above: A fully fueled and loaded jet can weigh up to 875,000 pounds.*

*Right: The wings of a 747 are big enough to fit forty-five cars on them. The wingspan stretches even further when the inner fuel tanks are full.*

This spread. The 747 rises into the air with its 875,000-pound-load of aluminum, fuel, passengers, and cargo.

Above: Four massive engines generate more than 250,000 pounds of thrust that lift the aircraft into the sky.

Right: The jets reach speeds of two hundred miles per hour as they lift off the runway.

These enormous planes get off the ground with the help of four engines that generate a total of more than 250,000 pounds of thrust, more power than seven F-18 fighter jets combined. Thanks to the physics of thrust and lift, when a 747 closes in on 200 miles per hour on the runway, a miracle called rotation occurs. And 875,000 pounds of aluminum, fuel, passengers, and cargo lift skyward.

Do not let the 747's bulk fool you. It is fast, too. This jet reaches speeds of up to 720 miles per hour during testing.

"It's the fastest subsonic commercial jet transport in the world," says Joe MacDonald, chief test pilot for the Boeing 747. "When we do testing, we are required to fly out to Mach .97, or 97 percent of the speed of sound. That's a very dynamic condition—it involves diving the airplane pretty sharply. And then you have to do maneuvers once you get to that Mach number. In some cases there has probably been, at least locally on the airplane, some supersonic flow."

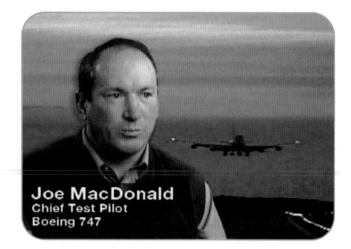

**Joe MacDonald**
Chief Test Pilot
Boeing 747

*Above: Joe MacDonald, chief test pilot for the Boeing 747, flies the subsonic commercial jet and reaches speeds of up to 720 miles per hour during tests. Below: Pilots are required to reach a speed of 97 percent of the speed of sound when they test the jets.*

*Right: It takes a lot to build the fastest and biggest jet in the world. More than 6 million parts must be assembled in the world's biggest building.*

*Left: Test pilots practice dives and special maneuvers to determine if the jet is ready to fly passengers for commercial airlines.*

The Boeing 747-400 is the fastest and the biggest, but those are not the only reasons this grand jet qualifies as a superstructure. It takes a city's worth of people, more than six million parts, and the world's biggest building to build the world's biggest jet.

## BUILDING A GIANT

When Boeing launched the 747 program in 1966, the company had yet to purchase the land the jets would be built on. Boeing finally selected a 773-acre site in Everett, Washington. The record-breaking jet was built just steps behind the record-breaking building that housed it. Workers started assembling the plane at one end of the building before the roof was on at the other end.

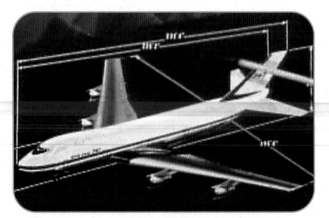

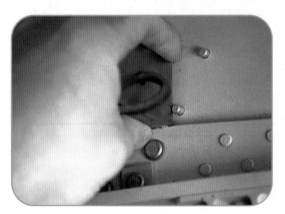

*Left: In 1966, without even having a place to construct its jets, Boeing launched its 747 program.*
*Below left: Workers constructed the world's biggest building, the Boeing manufacturing plant, on a 773-acre lot in Everett, Washington.*
*Below right: Even as construction continued in parts of the building, workers in completed sections began to build airplanes.*

Today, the building sprawls over ninety-eight acres—enough space for 911 professional basketball courts. This place has held fast to the record for the world's largest building by volume for more than thirty years. Inside, it is a small city, with its own fire department, medical staff, and food service. One urban legend has it that this structure houses its own weather patterns.

*Above: The finished Boeing factory covers ninety-eight acres and has reigned as the world's largest building for more than thirty years.*

*Right: A small city exists inside the enormous plant, including medical staff, food services, and even its own fire department.*

9:51
MAR. 9 1990

*Below: Jack Jones, director of 747 manufacturing at the Boeing plant, and his team can build a jet ready for the skies in just four and a half months.*

Jack Jones
Director of Manufacturing
Boeing 747

*Above: Ships, trains, and trucks transport more than 6 million airplane parts from all over the world to the Boeing plant.*

An aluminum avalanche of jet parts pours into this behemoth building, brought by cargo ship, train, truck, and cargo-carrying 747s. Some 670 vendors from all over the world supply the more than 6 million parts that eventually become a Boeing 747-400. More than half of those 6 million parts are fasteners—from the lowly rivet, a mighty jet is born. And there is an element of pride among the more than one thousand factory workers whose job is to transform parts on pallets into jumbo jets.

"We're pretty proud of how fast we can actually build a 747," says Jack Jones, director of manufacturing for the 747-400. "From the time the very first part comes into the factory to the time we deliver the plane to an airline customer, it's approximately four and a half months."

In those four and a half months, panels of prefabricated aluminum become sub-assemblies, like wings, tail sections, and fuselage parts. Those parts are then put together during the night shift in an exacting process called "final body join."

The final body join could not happen, indeed the jet could not be built, without a sort of highway in the sky—thirty-one miles of tracks, nine stories above the factory floor, where eighteen cranes, some capable of carrying forty tons, move jet parts to their places. The network is so big it requires its own control tower.

*Top right: The wings and other major parts of the jet are assembled separately.*

*Middle: Workers on the night shift put together the sub-assemblies in the "final body join."*

*Bottom: Cranes and tracks that run on thirty-one miles of tracks high above the ground help move these heavy sections.*

"We call it the 'dance in the sky,'" says Jones. "If you were look in at one or two o'clock in the morning on a line-move night, you'd see things flying all over the place. It's a real choreography."

Merging massive fuselage panels with microscopic precision was once a matter of moving slowly and eye-balling the gap. Today, a digital design system called CATIA, which stands for Computer Aided Three-Dimensional Interactive Applications, helps standardize the 747's fuselage parts and makes joining them a more precise process. Jones compares it to putting Legos together.

*Top: Tight organization and skillful choreography are necessary when eighteen massive cranes and their operators piece together the airplane parts. Left: Employees oversee a computer system that helps to join the fuselage panels accurately.*

This page: The construction process of a 747 jet is similar to piecing Legos together. Each part fits together with another to make a very large aircraft.

After the final body join, workers attach and test internal systems, replace fourteen-thousand-pound cement blocks with actual engines, and add other final touches prior to painting. Boeing began experimenting at the end of 2001 with building the 747-400 on a moving line. The company hopes to make the process more efficient by having the jets move constantly at a rate of one foot per hour through the final stages of assembly.

*Top: Workers replace fourteen-thousand-pound cement blocks with the jet's actual engines after the final body join.*

*Below: Boeing hopes to make the production process more efficient with a new moving assembly line.*

*Above: Workers test all the internal systems after the final body join.*

Almost complete 747-400s leave the final assembly building at the rate of one every eight nights, which gives an idea of how tightly this production schedule must be managed. The jumbos are usually pulled from the assembly building and towed over to the paint building during the dead of night. The jets must travel over Washington State Route 526

on an overpass, and the spectacle would likely back up traffic for miles if it occurred during daylight.

During the paint process, the 747 loses its green-tinted coating of protective vinyl and gains about twelve hundred pounds of paint. Then the nearly finished jumbo jet takes its place on the flight line, where it awaits its first flight.

*Above left: Every eight nights, workers tow a completed jet from the final assembly building to the paint hangar. There, the plane receives its final touch-ups and coatings of paint.*

*Left: Workers apply about twelve hundred pounds of paint to the 747 before it takes its place on the flight line. The aircraft's first flight is then just around the corner.*

## INTO THE AIR

The first time the giant jet takes to the skies, it is flown by a Boeing test pilot. That first flight is called a B1 flight. After a successful B1 flight comes the customer, or C1, flight. For this 747, a new passenger jet for the German airline Lufthansa, Captain Werner Meierhofer does the honors. Kicking the tires of a brand new 747-400 is one of his favorite job duties. He calls the plane the "queen of the skies."

*Left: The customer's first flight, or the C1, follows the jet's very first test flight, the B1.*

*Right: Captain Werner Meierhofer is one of the pilots who test new 747s for Lufthansa, a German airline.*

Capt. Werner Meierhofer
Pilot
Lufthansa

Boeing 747-400s cost between $180 million and $200 million, and customers inspect their investments inside and out before finalizing their purchase. Everything from vital systems like engines to cosmetic details invisible to the untrained eye is given

the white glove treatment. This jumbo sails smoothly through its inspection flights, which means it will be delivered on schedule.

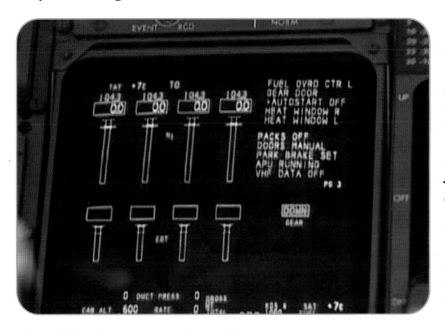

*Top: Customers must be prepared to pay between $180 million and $200 million for a Boeing 747-400.*

*Left: Buyers only finalize their purchases after they have thoroughly inspected every part of the massive jets, including engines and tiny details.*

*Right: A lot of work goes into preparing the finished jet for sale, including dealing with international banks, customs, and complicated taxes.*

*Above left: A new Boeing jet waits in the delivery area before it flies to its new home with the Lufthansa fleet.*

*Above right: Captain Meierhofer boards his jet, ready for the long flight from Washington state to Frankfurt, Germany.*

*Above: A testament to Boeing's vision, a new 747 takes to the skies and leaves Everett and Paine Field behind.*

Final delivery is more about moving money than moving jets. Imagine buying a $200,000 dollar house. Multiply the cost of the house by a thousand, involve international banks and customs agencies, apply local, state and federal taxes, and you have an idea of how complicated the final transaction is.

Finally, the deal is done. Boeing's one thousand two hundred and ninety-third 747 becomes the newest addition to Lufthansa's fleet. The ink on the paper is still wet as Captain Meierhofer takes the brand-new jet from its western Washington birthplace to its new home in Frankfurt, Germany.

No matter what role a person plays in bringing the jet to its final takeoff from Paine Field in Everett, the moment it leaves is as grand as the jet itself. Every time a brand new 747-400 takes to the skies, it is a testament to this company's vision

# ORIGINS

The origins of the 747's design go back to World War II and Boeing's military bombers—in particular, the B-47, the first swept-wing jet bomber. The origins of the 747's purpose go back to Boeing's dominance in the passenger airline industry. Boeing's ten-passenger model 247 was dubbed the first modern passenger airliner when it debuted in 1933. Propeller planes got people where they needed to fly until Boeing introduced the first jet passenger liner in 1954. The 707, or dash 80, is the queen mother of all modern Boeing commercial jets.

*Above left: Boeing originally created B-47 bombers during World War II. Later, the company used the design of the military bomber as a basis for passenger aircraft.*

*Left: In 1933, Boeing introduced the 247 as the first modern passenger airliner. The plane had a capacity for only ten passengers.*

*Above: Boeing unveiled the 120-passenger 707 in 1954. The first jet passenger liner set the stage for today's commercial jets. Below Left: By the 1960s, the 707 was no longer big enough to keep up with passenger demand. Right: Guy Norris cites the booming economy and growing population as why the world was ready for the 747.*

"In the 1960's, the development of the jet airliner came into its own," notes Guy Norris, West Coast editor of *Flight International Magazine*. The world economy was booming. The population was growing. And passenger demand for jet travel was rocketing at the rate of 15 percent a year. Suddenly the Boeing 707, which carried 120 passengers, just wasn't big enough anymore. Says Norris, "The airlines were feeling the onslaught of this great demand, and started knocking on Boeing's door to say, 'Hey, we want something bigger.'"

Guy Norris
West Coast Editor
Flight International Magazine

Juan Trippe, chairman of the then-industry-giant Pan American, knocked the loudest in 1966. If Boeing could develop a jet that could carry 350 passengers at Mach .9 on transoceanic routes, Pan Am would buy.

There were people who doubted this jet would ever fly. But to Joe Sutter, who was director of engineering on the 747 program and is thought of today as the father of the jumbo jet, the big question was what the airplane would look like. Two early designs were a double-decker jet, and a wide-body jet nicknamed "the Anteater." Today's jet more closely resembles the Anteater, with its wide body and a flight deck separate from the main deck cabin area.

**Joe Sutter**
Director of Engineering
747 Program

*Above: Joe Sutter is the father of the jumbo jet and helped design the original 747.*

*Below: Today's 747 is similar to the Anteater, a 1960s jet design with a wide body, separate flight deck, and main deck cabins.*

And what about the 747's most distinctive feature, the hump? "The rumor that the hump is there so the pilot can sit on his wallet isn't true," says Sutter. "It arose from the fact that we wanted to make a freighter airplane. We put the cockpit above the main deck so we could have nose-end loading."

Today the 747 has the distinction of carrying more cargo than any other jet in the world. It has carried everything from whales, to oil-drilling equipment, to a fleet of racehorses.

*Above: The unique hump of the 747 allows the craft to have nose-end loading, which lets passengers board at the front of the plane. Left: The jumbo jet carries more cargo than any other jet, and has even transported whales and racehorses.*

*Left: The first 747s had a double deck. Premium travelers enjoyed the lounge on the upper deck.*

*Below: Special four-legged landing gear ensured a safe landing even if other systems failed.*

The first 747s would have another cachet. The upper deck would be used as a lounge for go-go travelers, complete with a slick, spiral staircase.

Safety would be paramount in the 747. Multiple redundancies were built in, from four separate hydraulic systems to four-legged landing gear, capable of safely landing should part of the system fail. And in perhaps the biggest stroke of engineering genius, the 747 was designed with an eye toward the future—the jet could be modified to absorb new technology as it developed. That hallmark would turn out to be far more important than the hump.

*Opposite page: The jumbo passenger jet was designed to easily upgrade in the future as new technology came to the forefront.*

# 747 NUMBER ONE

On a wet February day in 1968, 747 Number One took off for the first time. Brien Wygle was copilot aboard the brand new jet.

"It was a great relief when we finally taxied out and everything was working and the engines were running fine," he recalls. "When we lifted off it set a great surge of emotion for us. We were busy so we didn't holler, but I think we looked at each other and grinned. Here was this huge airplane that a lot of people didn't think could get in the air.... And it flew beautifully, came back, landed beautifully, and taxied in. It's just a pilot's dream."

*Right: Finally, the aircraft so many did not believe in had a beautiful first flight through the skies.*

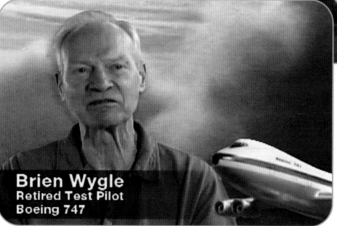

Brien Wygle
Retired Test Pilot
Boeing 747

*Left: Brien Wygle piloted the 747 Number One's first flight in February 1968.*

That successful first flight marked the beginning of a rigorous and dangerous phase of the jet's development, flight-testing. One of the first kinks engineers worked out was a problem called flutter, where the jet's wings vibrate at high speeds. The brand new Pratt and Whitney JT-9D engines presented other problems. "During the testing phase, we actually wrecked 64 engines," director of engineering Joe Sutter says. "These were severe failures—fan shafts breaking, turbine blades burning out, surges. There were a lot of problems to solve."

*Above: Flight testing can be dangerous if problems occur. One of the jet's first issues was a flutter, the vibration of the jet's wings at high speeds.*

*Right: Sixty-four engines were ruined during the 747's testing phase when turbine blades, fan shafts, and surges failed.*

Testing was, and still is, an expensive process of controlled destruction. New jets are pushed to the absolute limits of their capacity in the air and on the ground. In one brake test, called a rejected takeoff, pilots accelerate at maximum weight and maximum speed, then stop

dead just prior to takeoff. Then they must sit for five minutes doing absolutely nothing while a ground crew assesses the situation, to simulate real-life conditions. Each test completely destroys a set of wheels, tires, and brakes, at a cost today of about $1 million.

*Above left: A jet's rejected takeoff test costs at least $1 million because it destroys a set of wheels, tires, and brakes.*

*Left: A controlled destruction test simulates a real-life situation in which pilots push the craft to its absolute limits in air and on the ground.*

This page: These expensive tests are important to the overall performance of the 747 because they ensure that all systems will run properly once the jet is in action.

The original five 747s were put through the most rigorous testing program ever performed on a civilian jet. Less than a year after that, in January of 1970, the first commercial Boeing 747 entered service for Pan Am, flying nonstop from New York to London.

The 747 became a bestseller, and almost immediately new models appeared. The 747-200, a structurally stronger version of the 100, came out in 1970. The 747-300, which its stretched upper deck and capacity for forty four more passengers, debuted in 1982.

The jet that started it all, 747 Number One, christened *City of Everett*, now awaits restoration in Seattle. Boeing kept this jet to use for testing. The four other original test jets are still operational. One was retrofitted as a cargo jet and flies to this day.

*Right: Pan American airlines bought the first commercial Boeing jet and initiated its nonstop flights from New York to London in January 1970.*

Jack Waddell
Brien Wygle
Jesse Wallick

"FIRST FLIGHT"
February 9, 1969

*Top left: Boeing built new models of the 747 throughout the 1970s and 1980s.*

*Above: The 747 Number One, the first one of its kind, will soon undergo restoration in Seattle.*

*Left: The best-selling jet became stronger with each model and grew to accommodate more passengers.*

## A NEW JET

Today, more than 15 million flights and 35 billion miles later, the Boeing 747 is a brand new jet. The 747-400s built in Boeing's Everett plant today carry more passengers, weigh 140,000 more pounds, and fly 3,000 miles farther than their predecessors. They also have innovations that simply didn't exist when the jet was first developed.

*Top: Today's 747s weigh more than 140,000 pounds and can fly three thousand miles farther than the earlier models.*

*Right: The 747-400 carries more passengers and feature state-of-the-art enhancements.*

Among the most visible differences on the 747-400 are winglets—tips that extend upward about six feet on the end of each wing, where they trap that would otherwise bleed off the end of the wing. The purpose, according to chief project engineer Marlene Nelson, is to make the wing more efficient. "The winglets provide a little extra range by increasing the effective lift of the wing," she says. They also allow the 400 to squeeze into a standard airport stall and still enjoy the benefits of a bigger wingspan.

*Left: The new winglets attached to the end of each wing give extra range and lift to the wings without adding excess size.*

*Right: Marlene Nelson, chief project engineer of the 747 program, praises the new winglets that help lift the jet's wings more effectively.*

Marlene Nelson
Chief Project Engineer
Boeing 747

The high-tech winglets are made of aluminum and light-weight composite developed by NASA. Ironically, they're installed in a very low-tech way. Boeing mechanic Corey Stalcup, better known as the "Winglet Guy," needs only a couple of helpers and a bright orange mallet to get the job done

Corey Stalcup
Winglet Installer
aka "Winglet Guy"

Big changes took place inside the 747-400 as well, especially on the flight deck. Older 747s were

*Top: Winglet installer Corey Stalcup uses a low-tech system to mount the tips.*

*Left: Stalcup hammers the lightweight aluminum winglets in place with a mallet.*

flown by three crewmembers—pilot, co-pilot, and flight engineer. But Boeing wanted a standardized cockpit, so flight crews could easily transition from one Boeing airplane to another. That meant going from three flight-crew members to two, eliminating the position of the flight engineer.

*Opposite page: Because computers now do the jobs that were once the flight engineer's, the flight crew of today's 747, consists of only two people, the pilot and copilot.*

Crews had to get used to the new cockpit's ability to do a lot of the tasks people once did. Computers on this jet could figure out the most efficient route, check tire pressure, even automatically land the jet. Digital cathode-ray instrument displays replaced dated electromechanical or steam gauges. And the 400s currently coming off the line are further improved, with more reliable liquid-crystal instrument displays.

Some numbers went down when the 747-400 was developed. Flight crews on older 747s had to monitor 971 lights, gauges, and switches. That number now stands at a more sensible 365. Decibels went down as well. The 400s have newer, faster, more efficient engines that meet stricter noise regulations. And these quieter engines can now take this jumbo jet more than eight thousand miles nonstop.

*Right: The 747-400's cockpits make use of technological advances to accomplish tasks that people once did. Computers can check tire pressure, automatically land the jet, and map out flight routes.*

*Left: The 747-400 can seat as many as 568 passengers. Also, travelers have more space for their carry-on luggage than ever before in the jet's overhead stowage bins.*

*Right: Baggage handlers who load the 747-400 work quickly and efficiently to put more than forty-two tons of luggage into the jet's cargo hold.*

The changes most customers notice are interior features. Some completely revamped 747-400 interiors can accommodate a whopping 568 passengers. Crew sleeping bunks were added behind the cockpit and above the ceiling in the tail section, since flights can last longer than sixteen hours. New fire resistant paneling was added. And bigger overhead stowage bins give the 400 more capacity per passenger than any other wide-bodied plane. In the cargo hold, the 747's handlers load more than forty-two tons of baggage onto the jet in less than seven minutes.

When you see this gigantic jet swallowing five and a half tons of food to feed hundreds of hungry passengers and guzzling 57,000 gallons of fuel to sustain itself, you understand why crew members fondly call this beast the Whale. For the record, the jet dwarfs the average blue whale, which weighs in at a paltry 250,000 pounds. Boeing's latest model, the 747-400-ER (for Extended Range) has a gross maximum weight of 910,000 pounds.

The massive weight is especially incredible when you consider the one handling characteristic noticed by almost all pilots: It's easy to land. Gentle landings are due in part to ground effect. The jet's massive size actually compresses the air beneath it as it gets closer to the ground, creating an invisible cushion that softens the landing.

## NEW JOBS, NEW CHALLENGES

The 747's most obvious claim to fame may be its size, but this jet's combination of prestige and versatility has landed it some pretty interesting jobs.

The most famous 747 is *Air Force One*. President Bill Clinton once remarked, "Everywhere I go in that airplane, I am the second most important celebrity. People really just want to see the plane." The

president's Boeing 747-200 is owned by the United States Air Force and has been fitted with everything from heat seeking missile protection to an air-to-air refueling system. This 747 could effectively serve as an airborne White House if something should happen to the real one.

*Above left: President Bill Clinton flew in 747* Air Force One *during his presidency. The famous aircraft is owned by the U.S. Air Force and has special security features.*

*Left:* Air Force One *is equipped with heat-seeking missile protection and an air-to-air refueling system so it can serve as an airborne White House.*

Another 747 piggybacked the space shuttle *Enterprise* for NASA in the late 1970's, during testing. These jets have even been recruited by the military to defend the country with lasers. The ABL (Airborne Laser) project is developing a modified 747 capable of blasting ballistic missiles out of the sky.

The Boeing 747 has maintained its status for more than three decades. Soon, though, the 747 will face a new competitor. Boeing's biggest rival, Airbus, is developing the A380, a mega-jumbo jet. Measuring in at 239 feet, with capacity for more than 600 passengers, this will be the first production jet to challenge the reign of the queen of the skies.

*Top right: In the late 1970s, a 747 piggy-backed space shuttle* Enterprise *for NASA tests. Middle: Some military 747s will be equipped with airborne lasers to defend the country. Bottom: The famous Boeing jet will soon have a new rival – the Airbus A380, a mega-jumbo jet that will hold more than six hundred people.*

This page: When Boeing originally made the 747, the company anticipated demand for more frequent travel to farther destinations.

Jeff Peace
VP and Gen. Manager
747 Program

Boeing is not handing over the crown yet. Jeff Peace, vice president and general manager of the 747 program, believes his plane has the edge: "The A380 is a different airplane than the 747. It's quite a bit larger, at 550 to 650 passengers. We believe that it's too big."

When Boeing developed the 747 thirty years ago, the company placed a bet on a future where more people would travel farther. That bet panned out, or perhaps the jet itself helped change the way we travel. Now Boeing is placing another bet—that people want more point-to-point travel, not the hub-to-hub system that exists now.

"We think that the world will grow up in point-to-point," says Peace. "They believe that the world will grow up with the same transportation infrastructure, and larger aircraft will be required. The world will tell us in a few years which one made the right bet."

*Top: Jeff Peace, vice president and general manager of the 747 program, believes that the new Airbus is too big and that the 747 will still have an edge over its competitor.*

*Left: Boeing will continue to make changes based on what travelers want, which could include a shift from point-to-point travel to hub-to-hub travel.*

Meanwhile, something else is happening that recalls the days when the 747 was first being developed. Boeing is once again developing a supersonic jet.

Do all of these changes in the industry spell the end of the 747? This jet has had an unprecedented run. But Boeing continues to tinker with the 747. A longer-range version is currently being tested, and customers are already lining up.

Guy Norris of Flight International predicts that demand will keep 747s flying for another fifty years. If that prediction is correct, the 747 may have to hand over its title as the biggest commercial jet in the skies, but it will likely gain another: longest lived. And a legacy like the one that continues to grow for the 747 doesn't come from being the biggest thing in the skies. It comes from the dedicated characters who built and continue to build a jet that they believe in.

*Above left: Boeing plans to create a supersonic jet that will surpass all previous airplane models. Above right: The 747 changes constantly to fit with the times. No matter what other models it develops, Boeing can always be proud of its first super structure – the 747 jumbo jet.*

# GLOSSARY

**Cachet**  great prestige

**CATIA**  Computer Aided Three Dimensional Interactive Applications

**Empennage**  the tail section of an airplane

**Final Body Join**  the final assembly of all of a plane's major parts

**Flutter**  the vibration of airplane wings at high speeds

**Fuselage**  the central body of an aircraft, which contains crew, passengers and cargo

**Ground Effect**  compression of the air beneath a descending large plane that softens landings

**Microscopic**  very small; visible only with the aid of a microscope

**Prefabricated**  made in advance

**Rotation**  when an aircraft rotates upward on its lateral axis at the point of takeoff

**Supersonic**  faster than the speed of sound

**Thrust**  the force produced by an aircraft engine that drives the plane forward

**Winglets**  tips that extend upward six feet on the end of each wing on newer 747s

# INDEX